THE WENDYS

THE WENDYS

Allison Benis White

Four Way Books
Tribeca

Library of Congress Cataloging-in-Publication Data

Names: Benis White, Allison, author.
Title: The Wendys / Allison Benis White.
Description: New York : Four Way Books, 2020.
Identifiers: LCCN 2019031741 | ISBN 9781945588426 (trade paperback)
Subjects: LCSH: Williams, Wendy Orlean, 1948-1998--Poetry. |
Mothers--Poetry. | Women--Violence against--Poetry. | Death--Poetry. |
Grief--Poetry. | Psychic trauma--Poetry.
Classification: LCC PS3602.E66346 A6 2020 | DDC 811/.6--dc23
LC record available at https://lccn.loc.gov/2019031741

This book is manufactured in the United States of America and printed on
acid-free paper.

Four Way Books is a not-for-profit literary press. We are grateful for the assistance
we receive from individual donors, public arts agencies, and private foundations.

This publication is made possible with public funds from the
National Endowment for the Arts

and from the New York State Council on the Arts, a state agency,

[clmp]

We are a proud member of the Community of Literary Magazines and Presses.

Contents

in memory of my mother, W

O. WILLIAMS

For me, much of the world makes no sense, but my feelings about what I am doing ring loud and clear to an inner ear and a place where there is no self, only calm.

—from the suicide note of Wendy O. Williams, lead singer of the Plasmatics

Dear W,

My mind will not cool.

A constellation of cigarettes in the dark—to blow a ring inside a larger ring was once a language, a lyric.

You sang, Take me, take me / across the universe.

A boat made of paper gliding on black ice, but you have already sailed without me.

Dear W,

The desire for calm especially—my hand curled around a star made of wood.

When cornered or held down, the body shakes to release energy.

Another way to explain this sentence—

A torn red dress in the snow, a voice bleeding through a dream.

Dear W,

For a fever, on my tongue, another ice cube.

Unable to sleep, I drove toward the mountains until the sky was cold and feathered, pressing down.

This is the ghost of the sickness: I am numb.

Lying on my back tonight humming, God hung from the ceiling like a chandelier.

Dear W,

Not light opening the mouth, not an abacus of pearls.

Say goodbye to the world, you sang hoarsely, half-dressed, lying on the stage.

Are you afraid of the howl in the skull cup filled with flowers?

A braid of glass down my back, like listening.

Dear W,

Diamond-shaped and once, leaning over a lit cake, my hair caught fire.

This is what we are: in a dark room, igniting.

I remember the gasp, and above my neck a serrated light—the wish for water, clarity.

It hurts to sing to you, to me.

Dear W,

And this: a torso without skin in a glass case at the museum.

And the other bodies posed as if dancing, or carrying their skin over one arm like a dress.

What kind of love is death? I'm asking.

Peeled down to my voice.

Dear W,

How your eyes in this picture, your mouth—

Thin and small, my first teeth, I remember, were kept in a red dish.

And the rose petal I sewed to a handkerchief—a mouth for the dead
to speak through.

Or is there nothing left to say without a body?

Without loneliness.

Dear W,

Or paper gathered on my knees in both hands—a bouquet.

As if this was useful, an offering to the impossible.

As if each page was a snow flower, a place to tell the truth about desire.

Here—these are still alive.

GIVEN

One can begin to imagine so many possibilities as to what befell this sleeping, injured, or dead character as she made her way through the woods at night.

—on Wendy Given's series of photographs (2009-2010)

The Track

Of course it is the absence
that is so beautiful.

Human or animal, the snow
will fall and cover her
tracks.

Maybe each word
is a footprint filling up
with snow.

I was here, meaning
I am disappearing.

The Shades

At first glance, the trunk
in the river looks like a body
floating face down, naked.

After you died, I saw
you everywhere, which is not
uncommon. Several times a day,
I'd say to myself, Her eyes
(skin, hands) like yours.

I'd say to myself, But not you,
until everyone became more
and more not you, until you were
no one, nowhere—meaning
everyone, everywhere.

Ignis Fatuus

It is possible to be
lovely in the dark.

A few thin trees
leaning toward
each other.

In ghost or pale
light, my fingers
on my lips.

If to speak is to die,
I will whisper.

If to speak is to die,
I will make
trees of my hands—

I will say nothing
by shivering, I will
say everything.

The Hunted

The wolf is not real anymore.

God is not real.

Take my hand, the song goes,
and walk with me.

No, to be alone
is better, to love the world
but not someone.

Better to say
to oneself, Walk
with me.

Better to be
two-headed, to ask
and reply, to die
when she dies.

Sheathe

Even in the dream,
we lie awake in the
dark, side by side.

When I ask
if you're dead, you say,
Alive in your mind.

And of the four truths,
I remember two: we are
alone, we will suffer.

It's no wonder
we cannot sleep.

We cannot die,
your cool hand
in my hand, carved
from ivory or ice.

Zero

Tell me what you see
now in the dark
when you look up.

Even the moon has a human
face—open-mouthed,
startled.

What is love but our need
to see another face?

Another body, her long black
sweater still hanging
in my closet.

Like the suicide note
in Japan still carved
into a tree.

Something to hold
after you read.

Eclipse

To abandon,
to cease to exist.

To consume another
briefly in your
darkness.

Do you feel
the anxiety in a certain
place in your body?

Below my
neck, in my sternum,
a little knife.

When the shadow
passes, does the body
still exist?

My hand on my
chest as if I, as if I
shot myself.

Abandon

Now the mind is blue
and endless.

Swimming to the
bottom of the pool
as a child
to retrieve a penny,
my dark spot.

I was alone
and dropped it
to retrieve it again.

A game of devotion.

Or resurrection, the face etched
in copper always turned
away.

Look at me
holding you
between my fingers
and letting go.

The Guide

If I could find her
I would lie down with her
on a bed narrow
as a coffin.

The last house
is the smallest house.

Even the skeleton
found doubled over,
the skeleton of her child
still inside her.

If I could keep one
eyelash in a glass box
in my mouth—

If I could say one thing
I could bear, in a language
made of air.

Waldgeist

The souls trapped
in the trees in Dante's forest
of suicides can only speak
when their branches are broken
as they bleed.

What else is language
now but injury: why did you
break me?

Why did you leave me?

And relief: to bleed
in one place, for one reason,
to say I failed to live
sanely on earth
without you.

TORRANCE

Six steps up she had to rest, her head down, her blond hair coiled on and over the banister. Air whistled painfully through her throat as if it had grown barbs.

—on Wendy Torrance, bludgeoned by her husband Jack in Stephen King's *The Shining*

Begin again. Terrified at night, I had to remove the book from my room. Again. *I think writing / is desire / not a form / of it.* Please. In this scene, in this scene, she is trying to breathe.

*

She is climbing the stairs with an axe (a sea of blood made of glass). What is a book? You will die. What is a book? I tore out the pages, left them like feathers scattered in my lap.

The axe is a wish. The feathers are a wish. The blood trickling down her face—the knife in his back as he mounts the stairs behind her *panting.* Every word on this page is a wish.

*

If you open your mouth, if a book is *the axe for the frozen sea inside us.* Once a man hit me so hard a fist of light splintered behind my eyes. It's been so long since I've slept through the night.

She is climbing the stairs in my mind. Louder. Boiling water and a woman's lungs compared to a wingspan. Louder. A book is a coffin. Hoarsely. A white sheet draped over the cage of being.

*

If you open the cage, if you open the book: she is climbing the stairs with two broken ribs. *If you do not breathe through writing, if you do not cry out.* Listen. You are reading my mind.

Begin again. I am drawing the black bird across my forehead. Please. Cool, wet, the ink runs in lines down my cheeks. Again. Bleeding in the rain like a sheet of music.

*

I don't know what else to do with my hands. *Right behind you*, he says through gritted teeth—her hands on the banister pulling her up the stairs. What is a book? Alive, alive.

You can speak of a writing sickness—black and lunatic, each word escaping the cage. Once I came to underneath a man with his hand over my mouth, a gash above my eye.

*

A book is a nightmare. Lower your voice. In her robe and slippers, climbing the stairs, the violence is a kind of dream. Lower. A feather not an axe. Hush. His breath on your back.

She is climbing the stairs to stay alive (he will die in my mind from boiling not ice). Kill him. Out loud: Kill him. If you open your eyes in the dark, the book ignites.

*

If *this endless white paper burns out one's eyes.* If you go blind all your life *(which is why one writes)* trying to find the words for sight, the violence of the blank page is light.

I am become death, the shatterer of worlds—I am climbing the stairs with her. You will die of reading. Please. You will die of writing. Again. What is a book? To survive.

COFFIELD

Somewhere along the way, she had met someone who was angry enough or perverted enough to consider her survival in the world insignificant.

—on 16-year-old Wendy Coffield, the first located victim of the Green River Killer in Kent, Washington

1.

Maybe our emptiness is unimaginable / to each other: I want to be buried in my wedding dress / near the water. Maybe your emptiness is my emptiness (the photograph of her body pulled from the river covered in a white sheet). If you feel / like you're going to faint, my mother says in the dream, lie down, lie down, before she melts / into a pool of water I try to collect with my mouth.

2.

Because it is easier to miss a stranger / with your mother's name, young and doomed. In Egypt, it was believed, upon arrival in heaven, the heart was weighed against / a feather. Pulled from the water in a red blouse with lace trim, unhemmed jeans—it is easier, easier. And if sin / weighed the heart down, if the heart weighed more / than a feather, it was devoured.

3.

Because they have finished hurting us, it is easier to miss / the dead (I am not finished). The outline / of a unicorn tattooed on her stomach, two butterflies above her breasts. Because they have finished (I am not finished), because nothing is real / until it ends.

4.

Something now inside the mind, a soft hum, a flicker—if I could whisper, He must have carried her / down the rocks into the water, into your mouth, your ear—I don't know / where this is going: fear, longing to consume, to be / consumed. I remember being sung to, rocked, the feeling of collapse: one body into another. I hope death is like this—

5.

Death is the price of love (it has already / happened): a red one-piece knotted at the back of my neck. Death is the price / of love (it has already happened): my mother opens her mouth / in the dream, shows me rows / of jagged teeth. I know she is going / to kill me, and after I cry, I relax into the last moments of having / her undivided attention.

6.

Because I have given up the idea of heaven / but not the name. When I say, Wendy, she replies, in the dream, There is no name for what happened to me. Because it is holy to name / our emptiness, to repeat the need: Wendy. Wendy, hurt me / with every word, please.

7.

Because the love / keeps breaking. According to the Aztecs, / heaven was broken into thirteen levels, each level ruled by a different deity— goddess of salt, goddess of lust, god of darkness, storms, disasters, and frost. Because the love keeps breaking—goddess of death, / god of thunder, earth, and rain—all this to say / I miss you and I'm afraid.

DARLING

Come back, Wendy, Wendy, Wendy.

—J.M. Barrie, *Peter Pan*

"And Wendy fluttered to the ground with an arrow in her breast."

Maybe this is the dream
                        of the dead bathed in milk—
        so many red feathers

in my mind. I remember being alive
                        as a child—on a towel in the grass,

            from a white plastic kettle,

                        I poured air into a cup,   two cups.

What else still   but to imagine heat, sugar, death.

                        We drank nothing

                and it was good.

"'A lady to take care of us at last,' said one of the twins, 'and you have killed her.'"

Smoothing the brain,

        holding a knife   to build another

  mother. Like a house in the trees,

           I wanted to believe in God

                  to be safe

              and have somewhere to go.

We are all the same   and inconsolable, legs twitching

        during the nightmare.   Please wake me up,

  press one finger between my eyes

           like a doorbell.

"Perhaps she is frightened at being dead."

Perhaps the cry, the electricity

before the mouth goes black,

glossy, and hollow.   Perhaps all singing

aspires to silence (I have nothing

left to say), to burn down

the house where the song began.

Perhaps the sizzle in the teeth,   the string

of smoke rising

from the lips, a hiss of opera, the last note (glittering)

sung but still   in the air, half-charred,

half-disappearing.

"He was begging Wendy to get better quickly, so that he could show her the mermaids."

The world asks us to live,   to imagine

their long red hair, the scales   covering their tails,

layers of dark green

sequins. It is the possibility

of being both   that is so appealing—

sick and beautiful,   alive and dead,   a woman and a fish

cut in half, cut in half,   sewn together.

Wendy, get better—

"But there was the arrow. He took it from [Wendy's] heart and faced his band."

If we live   more than once, we must collect

sounds like nails

hammered to a wall, hanging images

on them afterward   for the next life

to memorize. Maybe

we have been here

forever and are tired   of being surprised: a snake carved from

silver coiled inside a red

box. We are not safe

and you will make

a beautiful bride.

"I will put a glass thing in her mouth."

There is no cure

but bleeding, and even then

the wings cut from the back

are still in conversation

with the body. Gone

deaf, I learned to tie

a black balloon   to each wrist, crush

pills with the back

of a spoon. To get high, meaning

to live on earth.

Finally, a kind of

quiet settles in the eyes,   then a wonder at my own hand

combing the air,

combing the hair

of nothing,

so slowly,

tenderly.

"Then he decided not to take his medicine, so as to grieve Wendy."

A ruby latch, a drop of blood

or glass (if the mourning   lasts forever), a black

penny flattened by a

train worn on a chain

around your neck (if the mourning

is a sickness),   half-erased and

smooth between your fingertips

as you lift it to your lips, if this

is a kiss, (if this

is a kiss), how blood

and love   taste like metal.

"Let us build a little house round her."

       Like a lemon peeled in a

spiral slowly enough   to make the longing

        holy,

           these are the words we were born

                     to say: curled

          around the knife   in one piece, the yellow skin

is the most natural

          prayer: Lord,

               destroy me

          carefully.

"Wonderful to relate, Wendy had raised her arm."

And the revelation: a sugar cube

in the palm   held out the window at night,   and the devil's

mouth, or the woman   pretending to be a horse:

her tongue, her wet bottom lip

as she takes it— the tingle on the skin

where the sugar had been.

If the living

are the dream of the dead,
Wendy—I am trying

to stay alive, I am feeding   a little sweetness

to the darkness.

"Pretty mother, pretty mother."

It is grief to come to in a black room

naming shades of blue: *royal, electric,*

sapphire. If speaking is a form

of crying   —*robin egg, ice, midnight*—

tell me the story of resurrection.

If speaking

is a form of crying,

I am lowering my mouth

over her mouth—

dark sky, turquoise,

water.

Notes

The poems in "GIVEN" are ekphrastic and each title is taken from
a photograph in Wendy Given's series, "On Myth and Magic" (2009-
2010)

In "TORRANCE," the italicized lines are attributed to the
following: Eileen Myles (31), Stephen King (32, 34), Franz Kafka (32,
36), Anaïs Nin (33), Marguerite Duras (35), J. Robert Oppenheimer
(37)

The titles in "DARLING" are taken from Chapter 6 of J.M. Barrie's
Peter Pan

Acknowledgments

Thank you to the editors of the following, in which some of these poems first appeared: *Bat City Review, The Best American Poetry: Poet Spotlight, HANDSOME, Los Angeles Review,* and *New England Review.*

Thank you to Martha Rhodes, Ryan Murphy, Bridget Bell, Lorene Delany-Ullman, Stefani Tewes, Jessica Treglia, and Steve White.

Allison Benis White is the author of *Please Bury Me in This*, winner of the Rilke Prize, and *Small Porcelain Head*, selected by Claudia Rankine for the Four Way Books Levis Prize in Poetry and named a finalist for the PEN Center USA Literary Award and the California Book Award. Her first book, *Self-Portrait with Crayon*, received the Cleveland State University Poetry Center Book Prize. Her poems have appeared in *American Poetry Review, New England Review, Ploughshares, Pushcart Prize XLI: Best of the Small Presses*, and elsewhere. She teaches at the University of California, Riverside.

Publication of this book was made possible by grants and donations. We are also grateful to those individuals who participated in our 2019 Build a Book Program. They are:

Anonymous (14), Sally Ball, Vincent Bell, Jan Bender-Zanoni, Laurel Blossom, Adam Bohannon, Lee Briccetti, Jane Martha Brox, Anthony Cappo, Carla & Steven Carlson, Andrea Cohen, Janet S. Crossen, Marjorie Deninger, Patrick Donnelly, Charles Douthat, Morgan Driscoll, Lynn Emanuel, Blas Falconer, Monica Ferrell, Joan Fishbein, Jennifer Franklin, Sarah Freligh, Helen Fremont & Donna Thagard, Ryan George, Panio Gianopoulos, Lauri Grossman, Julia Guez, Naomi Guttman & Jonathan Mead, Steven Haas, Bill & Cam Hardy, Lori Hauser, Bill Holgate, Deming Holleran, Piotr Holysz, Nathaniel Hutner, Elizabeth Jackson, Rebecca Kaiser Gibson, Dorothy Tapper Goldman, Voki Kalfayan, David Lee, Howard Levy, Owen Lewis, Jennifer Litt, Sara London & Dean Albarelli, David Long, Ralph & Mary Ann Lowen, Jacquelyn Malone, Fred Marchant, Donna Masini, Louise Mathias, Catherine McArthur, Nathan McClain, Richard McCormick, Kamilah Aisha Moon, James Moore, Beth Morris, John Murillo & Nicole Sealey, Kimberly Nunes, Rebecca Okrent, Jill Pearlman, Marcia & Chris Pelletiere, Maya Pindyck, Megan Pinto, Barbara Preminger, Kevin Prufer, Martha Rhodes, Paula Rhodes, Silvia Rosales, Linda Safyan, Peter & Jill Schireson, Jason Schneiderman, Roni & Richard Schotter, Jane Scovell, Andrew Seligsohn & Martina Anderson, Soraya Shalforoosh, Julie A. Sheehan, James Snyder & Krista Fragos, Alice St. Claire-Long, Megan Staffel, Marjorie & Lew Tesser, Boris Thomas, Pauline Uchmanowicz, Connie Voisine, Martha Webster & Robert Fuentes, Calvin Wei, Bill Wenthe, Allison Benis White, Michelle Whittaker, Rachel Wolff, and Anton Yakovlev.